# *Wrapped In Skin*

*Justin Jamar*

**The Elevation Project Creative**

Published By: The Elevation Project Creative
For additional copies of this book please visit:
www.wrappedinskin.com
ISBN-13: 978-0692401958 (The Elevation Project Creative)
ISBN-10: 0692401954

## *Acknowledgements*

Debra, Margaret, & Tammy
Forever and always, my protectors and my Angels.

This book is dedicated to my brother Jason. You are my inspiration everyday of my life. You give me strength when I start to believe that things will simply not work out. You have supported me in any and every endeavor I have attempted. You are the darker side of the moon; the side that no one sees but is necessary for its existence. I still want to be just like you when I grow up!

# Contents

## *Preface*

There is a reason for your existence. If you have ever associated the word "accident" with your life, now is the moment that you realize your life is not a mere accident. You wake up. You feel. You love. You hurt. You breathe. You were born for a reason. These are some of the things my mother told me as a child. Those words resonated with me so much, even back then. They gave me this warm feeling inside; I used to say it felt like I had swallowed a fire-fly.

My mother wasn't a highly educated woman in the traditional sense of the word. As a matter of fact, she had no formal education past high school, but one thing she seemed to know with her whole heart, was that her kids were special. She made me feel special everyday; as if I were made of gold. She knew one thing for certain, that God had given her specific instructions on how to raise two boys and she was going to do everything within her power to raise us with love and instill in us a sense of purpose.

I gave my mother a bible as a Christmas gift when I was eleven years old. She always wanted a bible that she could use to study, and there had just been a version printed called "The Living Bible". It translated the traditional King James Version of the bible into more layman's terms. She absolutely loved that bible and took it with her everywhere she went. She would spend hours at night highlighting and underlining scriptures; reading and rereading the text, all while making very small and carefully crafted notes in between the lines of scripture and in the margins of the pages. I remember thinking, "Wow, she sure is doing a lot of studying". It was as if she was preparing herself for something. Years later, I still have that bible and everytime I open it I get an understanding of what she was doing on all of those long nights. She was leaving notes and instructions for me. Each time I need to be informed or uplifted, I can open up that book and see a note that my mother left for me; as if she had known that one day I would come to that particular crossroad and although she wouldn't be here to tell me directly what I should do, she could leave her words behind to guide me. Although she didn't live long enough to see this book come to fruition, she started writing the text way before I picked up a pen. It is because of her that I write these words and ultimately this book.

For a long time, my EGO stood in the way of my writing. From the moment I began writing this book, I was forced to explore the depths of my spirit as I had never done before. It forced me to look at my life and how I was currently living it. It challenged me to be the person who I was always meant to become and that version of me sometimes didn't coincide with the person I was. My life, like many of our lives, was being shaped by the world and its expectations. I was living life through a "worldly lense" with an "earthly focus". I had become a product of my environment and it had shaped me instead of me shaping it.

One of my favorite authors, Dr. Wayne Dyer, says that E.G.O. stands for Edging God Out. From the moment that we are born, we begin to form an EGO. EGO can be defined as; *"the part of the psychic apparatus that experiences and reacts to the outside world and thus mediates between the primitive drives of human beings and the demands of the social and physical environment".* What this means is that, from the date and time that you see on your birth certificate, you began to be immediately shaped by the world, by your parents, your relatives, and your environment. Your psyche began to adapt and conform to the outside world so much so that soon your identity in God was lost.

We catch glimpses of who we were designed to be all throughout our lives. There are moments when we hear a faint voice, get a feeling in the deep recesses of our beings, or briefly notice the greatness within us. Some of us grasp onto it and hold on tight enough to reconnect and live a purposeful life. Some of us never find our way back to our true selves and are forever lost, seeking our identity in a world that is only meant to be temporary.

This is not a book about religion. It is a book about relationship; the one that your spirit and mine has with God. It is a book about becoming yourself as God saw you before you emerged into this world. It is a book about your earthly mandate, your mission, your purpose, and your birthright. At some point, in our effort to find our way back to God through religion or other endeavors, we have forgotten to focus on the idea of purpose. Many of us strive to live a sin-free life but not for the right reasons. To live a moral and righteous life helps you to achieve your earthly purpose. To live sin-free with no purpose was never the intention. It is my hope that by reminding people of their relationship with God and of the depths to which it goes, I will help them begin the process of re-connecting with the mission for which they were chosen.

The responsibility of bringing this book to life has been challenging for me on so many levels. I believe, however, that as long as I am connected to God I can accomplish anything. With this being the case, I hold on tight and I write.

*"There is a life in the crowd, and perhaps just one, who needs me. If my words find their way to them, then my life has indeed been worth the living."*

*- Justin Jamar*

### *Introduction*

There is an overwhelming consensus that we have a spirit; we are not just bags of skin and bones. Before I go any further, I want to make this one thing clear; my belief is that we should all grasp onto the understanding that we are not bodies with a spirit, but that we are indeed spirits who have a body. *Wrapped in Skin* is a journey of self-discovery. It is a journey that will lead you to the realization that we are spiritual beings having transformative, human experiences. There is a fire that burns inside of each and every human vessel. It urges us to push forward, to get up every morning and "go". It is what I call "The Push Power". It is this drive on the inside of each and every human that pushes us through the day, through the week, and through the years as if there is something that needs to be done; something that needs to be accomplished. We strive everyday to satisfy this urge with mostly trivial things such as our jobs, our hobbies, and even our friends and family. Perhaps you have even picked up this book to try to satisfy your inner push. Congratulations, you have landed on the right path.

This book is based on beginnings and origins. Everything has a genesis; a beginning. Your spirit has a genesis but where did it originate and why? Is there a God and did He create us? If He created us, then did He place us here on Earth? How old are our spirits? These are questions that many of us have had over the course of our individual human existence. The only thing we seem to know for sure is that our physical body begins to take form in our mother's womb, but when was our spirit placed inside of it? How long did that spirit live with God at its origin before He decided that it was strong enough to live on earth and carry out its purpose according to His plan? I would like to propose this idea to you; *Your spiritual life didn't begin with physical conception; the house, your body, was being built before you moved in.* When the Builder decided that the house fit the needs of the particular tenant, He allowed our spirits to move in. This is the part that we often miss, He moved us in and gave us a mandate. We often call this mandate "purpose", and each of us has one. Your body is simply the vehicle through which you will carry out that mandate.

Spirituality is spoken of in such a passive manner. It is paramount to our existence that we begin to comprehend the full weight of what spirituality is and what it means to be a spiritual being having human experiences. There is no denying the awesome power of God. We see His work everyday in the magnificence of creation and life. He is our origin. Our spiritual power emanates from Him. When I counsel and teach people, I often tell them, "Don't limit God by seeing limitations in yourself". What is impossible for God? The answer is, absolutely nothing. Let's say that you accept this book's premise; that God has sent us here with specific purposes. The next question becomes, if nothing is impossible for God, and He sent you here, then what is impossible for you if God is working through you? ALL things are possible through your divine relationship with God.

God speaks to me everyday and everyday He lets me know that I exist in this human form for a reason; there is a dynamic purpose attached to my life. He tells me this everyday because as many times as he says it, I still seem to forget from time to time. We sometimes have those "dumpster moments"when we are stuck so deep in a rut that it is hard to believe that we are great and that God trusts us with this life He has given us; with the gifts that He has placed inside. It is at these times that we need to slow down and remind ourselves of the infinite power that we are connected to. This power is always available to us if we would learn to plug into it.

I imagine that the strength of God's voice is unfamiliar to the majority of us. We sometimes struggle with the questions, "Does God hear me?" and "Does He care enough to talk back to me?". We can all agree that the further we move away from the origin of a thing, the harder it is to see or hear it. For example; my mother used to tell me to be a good boy in class and not to talk while I was there. When she told me, I heard her loud and clear and had every intention of being obedient; but when the moment came that I felt the urge to talk and disrupt class, I could no longer hear her voice as loudly. Before long I was able to block it out altogether. You see, I had gotten too far away from the origin of the mandate to really allow it to govern me. So too, is our spiritual relationship with God; we have retreated so far away from our creator that we have forgotten His face, His voice, His touch, and His instructions.

There are specific gifts and talents that we were given to help us complete our tasks. In addition to those gifts and talents, God gives us weapons I like to call "The Weapons of The Spirit". These weapons are so important! I will teach you how and when to use them to complete your task. My upcoming book entitled, *Weapons of The Spirit,* dives into these weapons using real-life examples of people who have become proficient with the use of them. Without a complete understanding of "The Weapons of The Spirit", we are fighting an uphill battle. It is not only important that we work to hone our life skills but it is also of utmost importance that we become proficient in the use of the W.O.T.S.

The majority of us are far more familiar with the "Weapons of Spiritual Destruction", thus focusing our life's energy on those things which take our power away. These weapons include fear, doubt, guilt, shame, regret, pride, hopelessness, and anger. These are very powerful tools and I can almost guarantee that if we look over the course of our life or the lives of our friends and family, we will find these weapons at work. People are often overtaken and consumed by one or more of these weapons. Every one of them can be like a nail from a high-powered nail gun, nailing us to the "wall of complacency." They can cause us to lead mundane lives, devoid of purpose; living in a perpetual state of impending doom.

God did not create us to die without living a meaningful life. This life was always meant to be temporary. Once our mission has been accomplished, God desires to have us back. We fear death because we never fully understand God's plan for our lives. Death was designed as our way back to God; it is our "Heavenly Rebirth".

We are the carriers of God's will here on Earth. We all have a gift, and no matter what, that gift cannot be taken away from us. The gift is wrapped up inside of us and although there might be an attack on the body that houses it, the gift is ours and ours alone. The power of our gift is only diminished by two things. One is if we refuse to use it. The second one is, if we choose to give it away and use it for something outside of the will of God, the one who gave it to us.

We hear stories and watch movies that follow the lives of undercover detectives. These are men and women who have shown a passion for the job in which they do. They have demonstrated a certain level of integrity and in doing so, have earned the trust of their superior officer. When things happen in a corrupt society, these men and women are often called upon to infiltrate the system by going undercover. These missions are often dangerous and could result in serious harm or even death to the person. Their superior officer often has his or her reservations about the mission but once the detective reassures them that this is a mission that they can and will carry out, the superior officer signs off on it and sends them on their way.

After he signs off on the mission and sends the detective on their way, the mission is just beginning. The detective is then briefed, highly trained, educated, and equipped with all of the tools that they will need to complete their mission. Often, shortly after going undercover, they begin to get so engulfed by the situations and circumstances in which they have been placed, that they soon forget, not only the mission at hand, but their original identity altogether. The longer they are undercover, the more difficult it becomes for their superior officer to contact them.

Likewise, we were equipped to carry out a mission on this Earth. This is a mission that we call "purpose". As much as God loved us in spirit, he knew that the world needed us to become human and carry out our purpose. He is constantly trying to reach us and remind us of the mission for which we were chosen. He tries to push us back on our "purpose path".

Some of these missions seem so daunting that we think they are impossible. While in this world, we have been conditioned to view ourselves as "only human". We are limited by the house in which we live. The way we approach life is equivalent to a person that will not step outside of their home for fear of what awaits them outside of those four walls. They have let the thing that was meant for shelter and protection, imprison them and keep them from achieving anything great or worthwhile.

It is my intention to help you rediscover God's original plan for your life. This is the very thing for which I was created; and although there is no way that I will be able to pull this mission off flawlessly, I will give it my all and I will stop at nothing to remind you that you are great beyond any measure that exists in this world. You were trusted by God to live a life of purpose.

This book is going to show you how to tap into God's awesome power and how to explore your spirit in ways that you never thought possible. Your true identity is hidden from physical sight but I have given you a road map in these pages to help you find yourself for the first time. You were intentionally designed the way you are for the purpose that God has attached to your life. You are completely capable of anything. Nothing is impossible for those who love God, love themselves, and live fearlessly while in this skin.

While wrapped up in this flesh, you have the ability to fulfill the will of God. Just as my mother told me when I was young, I am telling you; there is a reason. You wake up, you feel, you love, you hurt, you breathe, you were born for a reason. Now, let's discover it!

Within each chapter of this book, you will find both **Morning and Evening *Meditations***. The meditations are essential for a complete understanding and subsequent use of the information provided in each chapter. Repetition of the meditations will allow you to completely immerse yourself in the concepts. You will discover that after doing the meditations for just a short period of time, they will become embedded in your spirit; and it is my hope that the concepts will begin to manifest themselves through your actions, thus allowing you to live the life that you not only desire, but the one that you were created to live!

## 1

## *A Divine Design - God's Epic Plan For Your Life*

*"Life is a gleam of time between two eternities"*
*- Thomas Carlyle*

Human existence defies almost all rationale. For thousands of years we have been attempting to explain the "Human Condition". Some of the greatest minds in the history of the world have attempted to explain God to humanity. It is so ironic to me that the creation endlessly attempts to explain the essence of its creator, because when we feel the need to explain God, we need look no further than ourselves. Spirituality is the aggressive journey into self-awareness. It is inside of each one of us that we will discover who God is.

Perfect and yet perfectly flawed, this is your human machine. You exist, you live, and you die. The questions are, and have always been, "how and why?". Is your existence just accidental? Did it all happen after one "Big Bang"? Attempting scientific comprehension of space, time, and creation is a futile mission. Our minds can only stretch so far in the effort of comprehension. Science is perceptual reality. This means that science is only as good as our current level of cognition. It's hard to perceive that the sun is 92,955,807 miles from the earth when you feel it so warmly on your skin. Human perception is limited, therefore so is science. At the point that our scientific mind fails us, our spirit needs to take over. One thing is certain; if we take our spirits out of the equation of the human condition, we would all be zombies. We would be no different from a robot, operating in a calculated way based on mental capacity without any emotion, empathy, or compassion.

A quantum physics professor at Yale University and a leading authority on the subject, was asked if he believed that there was a God. Was there something or someone from which the universe emanates? He answered, that with all of his training and research, it is impossible for him to deny the existence of God.

Everything about human life screams of a creator. We are emotional and expressive creations. We feel deeply about our relationships and about the world around us. Humanity is the expressionary essence of God's infinite love. Joy, pleasure, laughter, and even emotional pain shows us that we are more than just a physical body.

John Polkinghorne, an English theoretical physicist and former professor of mathematical physics at Cambridge University, had this to say on the subject of God's existence; *"God's existence cannot be demonstrated in a 'logically' coercive way (anymore than His non-existence can) but theism makes abundantly more sense of the world than does atheism"*.

Polkinghorne quotes Freeman Dyson, another theoretical physicist and former physics professor at Cornell University in further explaining his position. He states, *"There is a universe which is the way it is in its anthropic fruitfulness because it is the expression of the purposive design of a creator, who has endowed it with the finely tuned potentiality for life"*.

Have you ever watched a baby sleep? Have you noticed

that they often laugh and smile in their sleep? Most dream psychologists say that dreams are repressed desires or manifestations of experiences that we have had. What then, could a newborn baby be dreaming about? If we assume that life starts at the birth of the human body, then a newborn baby would have very few experiences to pull into their dream state. What they are dreaming about is a place in their memory that we have long suppressed. They are dreaming about a euphoric place somewhere in the presence of God, before their spirit was placed inside of a human body.

If you are caught off-guard by this, it is to be expected. I want you to open your mind to your pre-human condition. We do not have the ability to comprehend our existence in a "post-human" form (although many religions speculate), neither do we have any greater ability to fully comprehend it in "pre-human" form. I believe the pre-human condition to be just as, if not more important, to beginning the process of trying to understand human existence. A look into the spirit of a child is often the closest most of us will get to grasping the concept of our pre-human condition. It is at this point in human development that we are closest to our origin. Babies know God intimately. They remember what it feels like to be in His presence. They remember the purposeful mandate given to their spirit. Have you noticed that babies have this wonderful built-in mechanism to distinguish happiness from sadness, content from malcontent, and equality from inequality? They pick up on these subtleties in human behavior without ever having to be taught them. Why is this?

The brilliant Greek philosopher Plato, had similar questions when he wrote about them in famous works such as *Meno* and his *Theory of Recollection*. At this young stage in human development, babies are more closely connected to their origin than some of us will ever be while living in this physical space called "life". It is my contention that babies are listening to God calmly reassuring them while they dream. He is reassuring them that He is with them every step of the way. He is letting them know that He is there and will be there always in all ways. I believe that this is one reason why children cry so much when they are abruptly awakened from their sleep. They are shaken away from an intimate communion with God and thrust back into the reality of an unfamiliar place.

A  purpose was given to you before physical creation began to take place inside of your mother's womb. Your purpose is yours and yours alone. Your physical body was created with this purpose in mind. Everything you need to fulfill your assignment, you already embody. What a profound discovery? To understand that once you have truly found your purpose in life, you can walk forward on that path with confidence, knowing that you were specifically designed to do this. Your human design is for your purpose. How much further could you get if you embraced this fact? If you understood that even the things you consider "flaws" in your physical body, are actually there to lend themselves to your particular purpose in life.

The following meditation reiterates what life is supposed to be. Repeat this meditation each morning.

## Morning Meditation #1

*Begin everyday with this one understanding and repeat aloud: "I was awakened today for a reason. Today my life has meaning. Every breath that I breathe is a gift from God. Every one of these breaths has been given to me in order that I may find my purpose and begin the process of living in it. Today I will seek to find and to fulfill my life's purpose".*

### *Remembering God*

You do not have to be afraid or doubt yourself. You are the embodiment of God's incredible idea. You don't even have to force the issue when it comes to discovering your purpose. God is not the author of confusion. When what you're doing with your life feels forced or confusing, you can be assured that, at some point, you have strayed off of your "purpose path". Perhaps you are attempting to live out someone else's spiritual assignment and not your own.

We often think "I don't know God and if He exists, he definitely doesn't know me". I want you to picture this scene; You stand before God. There is this incredible feeling of warmth, calmness, and comfort. Every word that God speaks sends vibrations throughout your being. It feels as though you're getting a massage up and down your spine but you don't exactly have what we could consider a physical body at this point. He is giving you your assignment. He is infusing you with His essence and encoded within it is all of the tools needed for you to live a full and complete life on earth; everything that you need to be full of joy and full of love, is being placed inside of your spirit. He breathes on you and you feel overwhelmed. He stands you up before Him and tells you that He will be with you every step of the way. You know Him intimately so you believe every word. He wraps you in His love and sends you on your way.

He continues to speak to you while you are in your mother's womb but already, even at this early stage of life, the world and its influence, is threatening your very existence; trying to get to you through your mother. She has a choice in all of this. She gets to decide how she will take care of herself and take care of you; or even if she is going to allow you a chance to be born and live out your purpose. God sends special protection to her. He works to keep her safe, while at the same time remembering His promise to her, that He would allow her to exercise "free will".

You hear God. He is still creating, trying to instruct your parents and moving parts to prepare for your arrival.

Finally, you are born into this world. The gift, your assignment, wrapped tightly inside of this bundle of skin. You have now officially entered hostile territory. The war for your soul and for your gift has officially begun but you don't realize that the war has started. You also don't realize that at certain points in this life, you will become a co-conspirator in the destruction of your gifts. There will be times when you second-guess yourself or when you involve yourself in destructive behavior. There will be times when you let fear, doubt, guilt, and shame get in the way of the things that you have planned. These are the times that you need to sit quietly and remember the sound of God's voice. You have to reassure yourself that God trusts you and that you are enough!

*"The soul always retains its ability to recollect what it once grasped when it was disembodied prior to its possessor's birth"*

*- Plato*

### *Sleeping Child*

*He speaks softly to the sleeping child*

*He says; "remember me, I am your creator, your lover, your friend"*

*The child smiles*

*He speaks softly to the sleeping child*

*He says; "remember me, I am your creator and I will never leave you nor*

*forsake you"*

*The child smiles*

*He speaks softly to the sleeping child*

*He says; "remember me, I gave you a gift"*

*The child wraps her arms around herself*

*He speaks softly to the sleeping child*

*He says; "remember me"*

*The world yells; "Wake up! I want to introduce you to fear, doubt, and*

*guilt"*

*The child cries and loosens her arms. She wakes up and runs to the world,*

*forgetting God and herself.*

## *Evening Meditation #1*

*Your objective is not to become who people think you should become, but to become yourself. Completely and fully develop into you. Trust, love, and focus on who that person is. Believe that there is a gift inside of you. Cultivate that gift so that when the time is right, you will be able to share it with the world.*

*Repeat this aloud:*

*"I will become the person that I was born to be. I will trust myself because God trusts me. I am good enough"*

## 2

## *The Birth of the E.G.O. - Edging God Out*

*"It is often the exterior of a piece of pottery that we marvel at. We notice its edges, its curves, and the beautiful paint. At one point or another, we will recognize that the true usefulness and essence of the pot lies in the space within it"*

*- Wayne Dyer*

We often harken back to the story of Adam and Eve when we try to explain God and His human creation. In the story of humanity's "fall from grace", the true disservice done by Adam and Eve (the biblical representations of the first humans) in their act of disobedience to God was that, with one act, they switched the design hierarchy of the human condition. By this I mean, it was at that very moment that human EGO began to take shape. Humans went from being spiritually connected to God and thus being governed by their spirits, to being led by their physical bodies. They succumbed to lust, desire, and worldly ambitions. They noticed their physical flaws and were embarrassed, trying desperately to cover themselves up. They, for the first time, experienced feelings of shame, guilt, and regret. This crippled and paralyzed their connection to God. Quickly, they **E**dged **G**od **O**ut of their lives all together.

From the moment you entered into this world, there were people around you catering to your every need. Their voices were loud. They all had opinions on how you should be taught, who should teach you, where you should go to school, what you should wear, so forth and so on. How many times did these people consult with God? After all, isn't it because of God that you are here in the first place? Let's go back to the previous chapter and think about how these voices and opinions are a huge detriment to God's purpose for your life. Before you know it, you are a teenager or a young adult and you have never reconnected with that God who you knew prior to being born. The assignment He gave you has been forgotten in a cloud of personal goals and ambitions. You have traded in your divine assignment for a life that the world approves of. You second guess who you are and you listen to the loud voices of the world that add to your doubts. They are like a loud chorus of boos, drowning out that voice inside of you that's imploring you to move toward your purpose.

Communication with God takes place mainly in your subconscious mind. Think of the subconscious mind as the storage room of everything that is currently not in your conscious mind. The subconscious mind stores all of your previous life experiences, your beliefs, your memories, your skills, all situations you've been through and all images you've ever seen. The conscious mind, however, is where the EGO resides. This is why it becomes dangerous to let your EGO take the lead. When the EGO takes the lead, it can often block out the voice of God. The EGO keeps you only concerned with pleasing yourself and the people around you, even if it's to the detriment of God's plan for your life.

God's voice exists in a different state of consciousness. It is something that you have to make an effort to tap into. You have to shut your conscious mind off at certain points throughout the day, whether it be through prayer and/or mediation, in order to open up those communication lines with God. This is what I call "Getting out of your own way". When you can lose yourself in order to find God, that's when you can really begin to communicate with the infinite power that is your creator.

Your EGO will keep you from recognizing when you are on your Purpose Path and when you are not. There are moments in life, if you look back over time, when you have done certain things that make you feel good. They make you feel as though you are doing what you are supposed to do. These things often come easy to you. You are not confused; you aren't having to force the issue. Has it ever occurred to you that these are the moments in which you have stumbled back onto your purpose path? Often times, what happens is that your EGO begins to tell you things such as , "That won't make you any money", "What makes you think you're good enough to do that?", "What will people say?". Your EGO introduces feelings of doubt, fear, and shame.  Once you let these feelings permeate your spirit, you jump off the road that you were traveling on and go do something that you deem to be "safer" or far less challenging.

Purpose is a "road less traveled" because it is YOUR road. No one else is on it but you. This is often a lonely road. It takes faith and courage to walk on it. You jump off because while you're on this road, you will have to be directed as to where to go. You can only see moment to moment at times and it takes faith to push forward into the darkness. It takes listening to a voice that, at times, might be faint and unfamiliar. It takes stepping into murky water, unsure of what lies beneath it. This is the road less traveled. It is often unpaved and filled with dirt. This road is yours, it has your name on it and you own it. Walk forward down it in confidence.

## *Morning Meditation #2*

*Yes, you are gifted. Do not second-guess your gifts. When you begin to operate in your purpose some things will begin to come easy for you. Sometimes they come so easy that you feel as though it should be easy to everyone else. This is the moment that you have to realize what God has given you. This is your gift to the world. All of us are depending upon you to do those things that you were born to do. Don't fall into the trap of believing that you aren't valuable. People need you. The world is the way it is because people need each other and some of us don't believe in ourselves and our gifts enough to share them with the world. Accept your gifts and allow them to grow so that you can become more confident and giving with them.*

*Repeat this aloud:*

*"The world needs me. I am necessary. My value cannot be measured by a monetary amount. I will cultivate my gifts so that I will be able to openly share them with the world."*

## *Embracing Your Gifts*

The best comparison I can find when it comes to describing why some people live lives outside of the will of God and thus outside of their purpose, is the experience that some undercover detectives have. Like undercover detectives, you were given a clear and direct assignment. Everything was prepared for you and you were prepared for the circumstances. At some point, you got so caught up into this "temporary life" that it started to consume you. You forgot your purpose and you neglected your gifts and talents. It became more important to you to please the world that you were suddenly thrust into, than to please the one who sent you here. You forgot His voice, making it very difficult to receive instructions from Him.

Some of us spend our entire lives either unable to hear from God or unwilling to listen. The good news is that God has built a mechanism within each one of us that lets us know when we have stumbled back onto our purpose paths. It's called *gratification*. Have you ever given some money to a homeless person, read a book to a child, or volunteered at a nursing home? If you have, you have likely experienced the feeling of gratification. This feeling is nothing that the world can give you. It comes from inside. It lets you know that what you are doing is righteous. Righteousness is simply a sum of behaviors that enrich human life. It is a consistency to your life that empowers and positively affects the lives of those around you.

When I was in college, I never really enjoyed studying (but what college student does?). It was boring to me. What I did enjoy was writing. I could write about any subject. I even liked the way the ink looked as it left my pen and spilled out onto the paper. If I had to write a paper, no matter what the subject, the feeling of gratification that I experienced from holding the completed paper in my hands was so euphoric. I really couldn't have cared less what grade I received on the paper, my reward was the feeling that raced through my spirit once I held it in my hands and could confidently say that it was finished.

This is a prime example of God trying to show me what it was that I was supposed to do with my life and an even better example of me letting my EGO and the voices of the world steer me in another direction. It would not be until almost a decade later that I would take time to cultivate the gift of writing that God had given me. It took years of trying to escape my purpose before I realized that what I was doing for a hobby was one of the very things that I had been sent here to do. Writing came easy to me, so in my mind, I must have been doing it wrong. Ideas and concepts constantly bombarded my spirit and mind. As often as God showed me His plan for my life, I told myself twice as much that it was a foolish thought. I didn't know any writers. I wasn't taking any high level english or journalism courses like some of the authors I had read. Anyway, I couldn't make money from being a writer. I had to get a "real job". I couldn't let my mother down.

Do these statements sound familiar to you? Aren't these some of the thoughts that have invaded your mind as you fight against your EGO? If you stop trying to force your agenda on God and allow Him to show you what He wants you to do with your life, I promise you, it will open up a whole new world. You will see things within yourself that you never thought were there, simply because you made a decision to embrace the vision that God has for your life.

# Evening Meditation #2

*Do not limit God by seeing limitations in yourself. You are the channel through which God's plans come to pass. Your job is to be available and useable. Your potential is unlimited. You can only fully tap into this limitless potential by allowing your instrument to be played by God. Give your life over to God and ask what His will is for it. Continue to ask Him and listen intently for the answer. Be aware that the answer could come from a variety of different places. Open yourself up to discovery. Let God lead you and take the guesswork out of your life. Your life is too valuable to just roll the dice.*

*Repeat Aloud:*

*"I am in complete submission to the will of God and the abilities of my spirit. I will embrace the things that feel gratifying to my spirit. I am open and available to receiving the signs of God. I seek to hear and understand the language that He speaks. I will live righteously so that my spirit can rise to the occasion and guide me through a life of purpose.*

*My potential is unlimited and I will receive all that God has for me in this life"*

# 3

# *The Voltron Epiphany - Spirit, Mind, Body Hierarchy*

*"Victory happens when the fighter on the outside lives up to the*

*expectations of the fighter on the inside"*

*- Justin Jamar*

God is the ultimate creator, the ultimate multi-tasker. He moves the pieces of my life and your life simultaneously; often allowing them to interact in miraculous ways. He is great at what He does and made us divinely magnificent. The work He has done in creating us seems so effortless that we begin to take credit for our own marvelous existence. It's like that movie *Rise of the Machines*. The machines began to try to underscore the efforts of their creator. We chalk miracles in our lives up to just mere coincidences. We begin to pride ourselves on our personal "success" in life. We get so caught up in the machine (our physical body) that we forget that we are who we are in spirit first. Each human body is a machine, a vessel. Each is different and of brilliant design. Each machine is specifically created for the challenges associated with its spirit's individual purpose.

As a kid, I used to watch this awesome cartoon called *Voltron*. It was a cartoon about a team of young space cadets that had been chosen to protect the planet earth from an evil, mutant invader. The way they were to go about doing this, was by utilizing the abilities of giant robot lions. Each of the lions was special in its own right. They each had a unique gift that none of the others possessed. Sure, they had weaknesses as well but their gifts were so great, that when properly utilized, they could easily overcome any deficiencies.

As magnificent as the lion robots were, they were nothing without the space cadet who was to become the pilot of the lion. You, being a spirit and God's epic idea, are the pilot. The body is nothing without the direction of the spirit, just as the robot lion was nothing without the space cadet.

Each space cadet fit with one individual lion like a glove. Once the cadet took hold of the controls, he or she could be almost unstoppable inside of the lion. The pilot of the green lion could not pilot the red lion and vice versa. Each one, specific for its given talents and skills according to its purpose on the team.

You command your body with glad thoughts, with proper nourishment, with care and love. If you do this, you can use it to do almost anything you want. It will become an unstoppable machine; it will become a lion.

By understanding their individual machine and following the plan of the "Lead Lion", The Voltron Force was always able to defeat the evil invader. In your case, God is the Lead Lion and He always has a plan. At times the situation looked dim for the team of young space cadets; but faith in their abilities, in one another, and in the plan of the leader always enabled them to have victory.

You and you alone, were chosen to power your machine. To do this, you must first recognize yourself as the pilot and not the machine. Your job is to utilize the capabilities of the machine in order to achieve your goal. Whether it's ridding the world of an evil invader as did the "Voltron Force", or curing the world of cancer; your purpose is yours and yours alone.

French Philosopher Rene' Descartes, formulated a philosophy that he called the *Theory of Dualism* in which he proposed the idea that the spirit and the mind are not inseparably attached to the physical body. The spirit exists in a separate space and thus is not subject to the same limitations of the physical environment. A strong spirit will supercede any perceived limitations of its physical environment. Remember, you are a spirit with a body, not the other way around.

Another way to think about the hierarchy of the human design is to look at it much the same way we look at a car. The car is powered by the motor in which everything runs off of. Without the motor, there is no car. The human motor is your spirit.

Secondly, a car has a transmission. This is the connection between the motor and the rest of the car. The transmission determines which direction the car travels (forward, reverse, or if it remains in neutral). Your mind is your transmission. You travel in the direction of your thoughts. It is what you consistently focus your mind on that determines the trajectory of your path.

Finally, the car has a body. This is the part of the car that people judge. This is what is immediately recognizable. The body of the car can either speak as a testament to the integrity of the entire vehicle or it can be made to cover up flaws and imperfections in the car's motor and transmission.

Your body acts in much the same way. The usefulness of the car is based on what's on the inside. You must nurture the spirit and the mind first. Once those two things are running smoothly, your body will follow suit. No one wants a great looking car that doesn't run.

## Morning Meditation #3

*Make absolutely no mistake about this next point. The body is the servant to the mind and the mind is a puppet on a string that is controlled by the spirit. Command your body with glad and beautiful thoughts. Keep a journal with you and chronicle every time a thought of illness, ill-content, malice, jealousy, anger, or the like enter into your consciousness. Write down where you are, what you are doing, who you are with, and even the time of day and day of the week. Try to identify patterns that lead you down this toxic path. By doing this you will be better equipped to keep thoughts such as these from entering into your mind and taking root in your body.*

*Repeat aloud:*

*"I am more than my body and I am better than my mind. I control them both. I am the captain of this ship. I will be physically and mentally strong. I do have good physical and mental health because I have decided that it is so. I will*

*command my body and my mind to do what they are supposed to do according to my purpose. I will take care of my body and I will cherish every aspect of my mind."*

## *Let Your Spirit Lead*

I have always known that at some point in this book there would be a need for me to share some personal stories. It is important for you to know that the lessons in this book are more than just theory. The words and ideas in these pages are a culmination of my own life experiences up to this point, as well as the experiences of some very important people in my life.

Growing up, I never really had a strong relationship with my father. I wouldn't call it a "bad" relationship, but it just wasn't an ideal vision of what a father-son relationship should be. My parents separated when I was four years old, so I really have no recollection of ever living in the same household with my father. I saw him often because I grew up in a really small town and he only lived 3 blocks away. Most of my early interaction with him was pushed on me by my mother. I adored my mother, so in my eyes, she could do no wrong. My brother and I were both taught at an early age that we were to honor and protect the women in our lives. As a young kid trying to figure out this whole "manhood" thing, I couldn't understand my father. It didn't make sense to me that he wouldn't do everything within his power and call upon every force outside of his power to be a true father to me. I couldn't understand why he had to live in a different house, why there was very little emotional connection between us, or why he wasn't there to show me how to ride a bike or cheer me on at football and basketball games. For this reason, I found myself often dismissive of his presence.

I can recall one time in particular when my father came by to see me. I was in the house (playing video games) when my mother, who was sitting out on the porch, called my name. In typical fashion I yelled back "Ma'am?" She said "come outside, your dad wants to see you". Now, I can't really tell you if my lack of interest in going outside had more to do with him or with the game of *Sonic the Hedgehog*, in which I was currently enthralled. Either way, I wanted no part of going outside to say hello to him. After a couple of minutes, my mother came inside to see why I hadn't made it out yet. She was also insistent that my father remain in the street because, according to her, "He hadn't earned the privilege of coming into the yard since he neither lived there nor had he ever paid a single mortgage payment."

That was my mom. She was a Godly and incredibly spiritual woman but she had a side of her that was so black and white and to the point. You crossed her at your own risk! She asked me why I hadn't made it outside yet. Now, I could have just told her that I wasn't finished with the game but there would have been a couple of problems with that. The first problem was, when my mother told you to do something, the only valid reason you had for not doing it was, if you were on your deathbed and couldn't move. In this case, the video game was completely irrelevant. Secondly, when it came to the subject of my father, I figured she would understand why I wouldn't want to see him. So I simply said, "I don't want to see him and why should I have to?" I remember her next words as if she said them to me yesterday. They are forever etched into my memory. She said, "Justin, let me tell you something. Your father and I don't get along and we probably never will, but that is something that we have to deal with. He is still your father and I don't want to ever see you disrespect him. Now go outside and see your daddy".

That moment changed my relationship with my father. She had given me something deeper to connect to. It stopped being about him and even about myself. It started being about the respect and honor I had for the woman who brought me into this world. She knew how important it was for me to have a relationship with my father. She was selfless; and cared enough about me to make sure that she never stood in the way of that.

Over the years, my father and I developed a pretty good relationship. The older I got and the more involved in sports I became, the more connected we grew. It was never a storybook relationship but it served us alright. In 2012 my father lost a brief battle with cancer. This story is important because of what I witnessed within my father during that time and what I would ultimately learn from his life.

He was one of those "old school", rugged guys. He

always had a chiseled physique but had never seen the inside of a health club. He ate whatever he wanted to and didn't gain an inch on his waist. He worked hard when he had a job and drank hard when he didn't have one. He chain smoked but would frequently quit for months, even years at a time.

Leading up to his diagnosis, he had several episodes of blacking out or getting really short of breath. The first time this happened he called me. It was the first time I had ever been able to recognize any sign of fear in my father. For the first time since he was a child, he felt out of control of his situation. Not to mention, we had lost my grandfather to similar symptoms that had turned out to be a heart condition.

The doctors discovered that he had a small blockage in one of his arteries. The surgeon was able to go in and fix it with a pretty cut and dry procedure. For a while he felt better. I would later come to realize that he felt better because his mind told him that the problem had been alleviated. This allowed him to override the effects that the real problem was having on his body.

Almost a year after his surgery, the symptoms returned.

This time, there was a more in-depth examination and the doctors discovered a tennis ball-sized tumor in his lung. This had been the real problem all along. I had never witnessed someone go downhill so fast. He literally went from one day being this strong, able-bodied man who had just made it through heart surgery, to the next day being confined to the couch. His voice became immediately shaky and he stopped eating. He lost about 30 pounds in 3-4 weeks. Following his diagnosis he had essentially resigned himself to the belief that this life was over for him.

This is a man who had probably lived with the disease undiagnosed for years. He was of strong mind and spirit. Although, the disease may have been attacking his body, it had no real power over him until it was able to reach his spirit and his mind. Within 3 months of his diagnosis, my father's time on this earth was over.

I am blessed to have had the opportunity to have him as a father. He taught me so much, some intentional lessons and some by accident. One of the biggest lessons he taught me was that you can't let your body lead. It will lead you to a place that you don't want to go. You must realize that your body will conform to the will of your spirit. My father never had to deal with sickness and because of that he never had to make a decision as to whether he would listen to his body or listen to his spirit. He also, never had this idea of the hierarchy of the human condition laid out in front of him. I truly believe that my father could have benefited from this book and that it would have been able to change or redirect his thoughts in a powerful way. Although the words in this book came after he left this physical space called "Life", I am so thankful to him that he has aided me in developing these concepts so that I can hopefully change the way you view your life and your human hierarchy.

Modern medicine is important and I am not denying its benefits. What I am saying is, we have more power to control our health than we give ourselves credit for. You are powerful beyond measure. Don't diminish your power by believing yourself to be at the mercy of your physical body.

## *Evening Meditation #3*

*All of the water in the world can't sink a ship unless it gets inside. Once you let negative thoughts and ideas permeate through your mind and ultimately flood into your spirit, you will truly watch your ship sink right before your very eyes. Work on plugging the holes in your spirit; the holes that appear over time by being bombarded with worldly situations. This doesn't mean that you go through life ignoring real issues. What it means is that you take back the power that you have over them.*

*Repeat aloud:*

*"I am great beyond measure. I am not my situation or my circumstances. I am more than it. It is because I am valuable to God and my life has meaning that I will overcome anything in my life that is trying to take me down. Wellness is within me and I am well"*

## 4

## *Unwrapping Your Gifts - It's Been Inside of You All Along*

*"Our deepest fear is not that we are inadequate. Our deepest fear is that we are powerful beyond measure. It is our light, not our darkness that most frightens us. We ask ourselves, Who am I to be brilliant, gorgeous, talented, fabulous? Actually, who are you not to be? You are a child of God. Your playing small does not serve the world. There is nothing enlightened about shrinking so that other people won't feel insecure around you. We are all meant to shine as children do. We were born to make manifest the glory of God that is within us. It's not just in some of us; it's in everyone. And as we let our own light shine, we unconsciously give other people permission to do the same. As we are liberated from our own fear, our presence automatically liberates others." - Marianne Williamson*

I remember when I first heard that quote by Marianne Williamson. I had no idea what it meant. How could we possibly fear greatness? How can our light be more frightening to us than darkness? Often, the quote is not read in its entirety. Because of this, I believe that we often miss the most important part of what Marianne was trying to tell us. The crux of the matter is that you are a child of God; the exact embodiment of what God is. Your playing small does not serve yourself, does not serve the world, and it definitely does not serve God and His intention for your life. We often times shrink ourselves in an attempt to evade judgement. We believe that if we quiet down and tuck ourselves away in a corner that no one will be able to judge us, ridicule us, or doubt us.

As I've told you already; you are special. You are exactly what you are supposed to be. You were created and designed because God saw fit to make you the way you are. He gave you a uniqueness that no one else can duplicate. The thing that you are supposed to give to the world is specific to you, so if you decide not to utilize those gifts, there is no doubt that the world will miss them. Suppressing your true gifts out of fear, shame, or doubt is to ignore God totally.

I was a very observant child. It always intrigued me how some kids were so different. I had a friend named Brandon who was one of the most charismatic people you would ever meet. He just had this thing about him that made everyone want to be around him. There was nothing special about him physically. In fact, he was a pretty wimpy kid. He was tall and skinny with long, lanky arms and legs. He wore his hair really scraggly and it was rarely, if ever, combed. Brandon, however, was like a magnet. He was intrinsically gifted with the unique ability to energize and galvanize people. Amongst our group of friends, I was kind of always the "leader". It was just sort of the natural order of things since we were old enough to walk. I was a little physically stronger (which is a necessity among boys who are trying to figure out what manhood is. Physical strength equaled manhood to us at that age) and I was a natural planner and organizer. Brandon used to tell me that he wished he could be like me in certain ways. I would never get the chance to tell him how much I admired his characteristics because of this little thing that I had developed even way back then called "pride". Even the ability that he had to open up and let his feelings be heard was very unique. He was fearless with his gifts and more importantly, he was unapologetic about them. He understood his shortcomings but he also knew that his gifts far outweighed them. Brandon was like a sharpened arrow. Except, instead of being launched through life by a bow that sent him in a definitive direction with force, he was like an arrow that had been thrown by hand. He often drifted in the wind, never really finding a set path. His choices weren't the best and it often got him into trouble.

When I first got the call that Brandon had died in a car accident, the first thing I recall thinking was how much we needed him and how many people would never have the opportunity to experience what he was supposed to give to the world. It was just a few days removed from his 21st birthday, and he was gone. I often wonder what things we are missing out on in his absence. I'm not sure I will ever know the answer to that question.

Lives are cut short every day as a result of making the wrong decision. Some of us live our lives thinking; "que sera sera" (whatever will be, will be). We believe that life and death are results of inevitability and not a result of choices; that our purpose, if we have one, will be fulfilled or not fulfilled regardless of the choices that we make.

There is a school of thought that wants us to believe that the outcome of our lives is out of our control. This is very misleading. Let's use, as an example, the street that you drive on every day when you leave your house. The street exists, just as your purpose exists. The choice to drive down the street rests completely in your hands. This doesn't diminish the value or the existence of the street but it does highlight the power of choice. Your purpose is there for you to grab ahold of, but the choice to pursue it rests squarely on your shoulders and no one else's.

It is not my intent to lead you to believe that each life is meant to be lived out to a ripe old age and that those who don't live to see their grandchildren or great grandchildren, stand any less of a chance of fulfilling their purpose than anyone else. What I am expressing to you is a sense of urgency that needs to be established in your heart. You should do what you can with what you have and expect nothing less than great things.

I had the honor of developing a friendship with another person who utilized his talents and gifts like no one else I have ever met. He lived each day with intention and with a fervent zest for life. When his life ended, he too left a void; a chasm in the lives of so many of us who had the pleasure of knowing him.

It was just before dawn on a brisk February day in Los Angeles when my phone rang; "DJ--what could he want at 5am?", I thought. I had been in LA for less than a week and it was 7am back at home (in Kentucky). DJ and I had gone to college together and worked at the same on-campus job but we weren't really that close until around graduate school when a mutual friend introduced us. Our friend Richie was a "master connector". He had this way of bringing people together regardless of race, class standing, political/social views, etc. We all liked each other and got along because we all liked Richie. I had only seen Richie in passing during undergraduate school. It wouldn't be until I returned to graduate school that our friendship would really blossom. I had been looking for a place to stay and a friend of mine suggested I talk to this guy named Cameron, who was looking to rent out a room. All I knew about him is that he needed a roommate and I needed a place to live. When I walked into the house, Richie was there hanging out. The next couple of hours that I would spend getting to know those two would help shape my life from that point on. They would become two of my best friends in the world.

Almost immediately from that day forward Richie and I became inseparable. There are people in your life who know things about you that know one else ever will; people who will have an impact on your life so profound that you would be hard-pressed to see where you would be if you had never known them. We partied together, we laughed together, and at times we cried together. I moved all over the country in my pursuits and there were a couple of people who I could always count on the come visit me no matter where I ended up; Richie was one of those people.

I hadn't told anyone that I was leaving for California except for my family. To be honest, I still hadn't come to grips with this crazy thing that I was doing. I called Richie about 2 weeks before I was to leave and told him that I was moving. He couldn't believe it, but he was absolutely ecstatic about it. He couldn't wait to visit LA.

I had seen him during the Holidays with his nephews. It seemed as though he had bought practically every toy in the mall. The smiles on his nephews' faces confirmed that they had gotten Uncle Richie to buy them everything they wanted and more. This was unusual for Richie. He believed in saving and investing; nothing flashy. He only bought what was absolutely necessary. He had an incredible job but he bought all of his suit jackets from the Goodwill. To him, not only was he saving money but he was also supporting a good cause. He had told me over Christmas that he was purchasing another house. I couldn't believe that a young guy who was unmarried with no kids was looking for an additional house when he seemed to be perfectly fine with the place he was in. I would later find out just how selfless he was.

I didn't answer the phone call that morning. DJ called again and I still didn't answer. This time he left a voicemail.

The lump in my throat right now as I write this was twice as big when I listened to the voicemail; "Its Richie man.....he's gone. He passed away last night". As unreal as it seemed and as much as I wanted to tell myself that this was either a mistake or a sick joke, something deeper in me knew better. It was the day after my birthday and my emotions couldn't have gone from one end of the spectrum to the other more quickly. I left my apartment and walked down the street not knowing where to go or what to do. I had so many thoughts rushing through my head; "How was I going to get the money for a flight home?", "Should I even go to the funeral?", "Why did this happen?", "Why to Richie?", "Who should I call?", "Why am I here?" (a question I would ask myself too many times to count while I was in Los Angeles).

Apparently, Richie had been having several health issues that he had told no one about. The extra time that he had been spending with his nephews was a direct result of him knowing that his time was short. The house he was purchasing, was to be left to his family in his will. He had taken out more than one life insurance policy on himself. He had worked harder at his job in the time leading up to that night than ever before. I thought, "How does a man who knows that the end of his life is near, stay so calm and faithful?" If I was the epitome of selfishness at that time, he was my antithesis.

This would be the first of several tragic losses I would experience during my time in LA. The other two would hit me even harder. I questioned God quite a bit during those moments. To question God is normal but don't be shocked when your mind can't comprehend the answer.

I am so fortunate to have known Richie. He taught me so much about myself and about people. He helped me cultivate relationships that I would need in my life. He showed me that every day is a gift. Every breath that you breathe is ordered by God. We must be obedient and good stewards over the life that God has given us. One day, if I'm lucky, I will be able to affect half as many people as my friend Richie did in his short time here on this earth.

Life is filled with traps and snares. You don't have time to sit on your hands and second-guess your greatness. You have to embrace your gifts and seek direction for how you are to use them. You have to be accountable for the decisions that you make each and everyday. You, along with God, are the co-creator of your destiny. We NEED you!

# Morning Meditation #4

*Who are you and what are your gifts? What comes easy for you but hard for other people? What in your life makes you feel as if you have swallowed a fire-fly once you do it? If you could do one thing and one thing only for the rest of your life, what would that one thing be? Don't consider any perceived consequences whether they be money, resources, other people's opinions, etc. Take as long as you need to answer these questions but please do not leave them unanswered.*

*Repeat this aloud:*

*"Who I am is great. I am more than ok. I will not worry about tomorrow because today, I am strong"*

### *Allow it to Breathe*

I had a conversation a few years back with a friend of mine named Tim. We were discussing the concept of "meaningful work"; the belief that what you are doing for a living not only makes a difference in the world, but it is also a part of what you were created to do or to become. Tim is one of those people who is convinced that his existence is merely coincidental. From what I have gathered from him over the years, he believes in God, but I think his mindset about God and creation changes from day to day. He doesn't believe that people have a definitive purpose for living. In his opinion, life is just happenstance. We would often get into these discussions about life and its meaning, due to certain issues that would come up related to his business. I have a background in human resources and at the time Tim was running a fairly successful business, but was having some issues with his employees. He had brought me in to help him with some things. As you can imagine, my approach to getting the most out of people is all centered around the reason for which they exist. Often, while speaking with his employees, I used real life examples and illustrations in order to get them to understand how to utilize their own gifts and talents. I'll share with you an example from Tim's own life that I have used with his employees and one that I still use often when speaking to people about how to identify their gifts.

Tim has a younger brother. The two of them were raised in the same household by the same parents. They are very close in age (roughly two years apart), but you could hangout with them for weeks at a time and if they never told you that they were brothers, you would not be able to tell just by watching and observing who they are as people. Tim is one of the most motivated and outgoing people you would ever meet. Even when he attempts to make a conscious effort to just settle into a groove and relax, you can tell that his spirit is unsettled. In college he was really involved on campus. He was President of his fraternity, helped organize freshman orientation, played intramural sports, you name it and he was involved in it. He has a remarkable way with words and is very energizing. He always has an idea for the next `` big business''. He is a "go-getter" to say the least.

His brother, on the other hand, couldn't care less about the public spotlight. If he could stay indoors all day he probably would. He and his wife live out in the middle of nowhere with their dogs and that's just the way they like it; but this guy can literally build anything. He can take your computer apart and put it back together one day, then start building a house for you the next day. He just doesn't want to have to talk to you while he's doing it.

My question to Tim has always been, "Doesn't a part of you think that these unique talents and abilities lend themselves to you and your brother's individual purpose in this life?" He often just waves me off but I like to believe that in private, he ponders this thought. One day I'm sure he will come around and seek to discover God's intention for his life.

Understanding your gifts is perhaps the most crucial part in achieving your purpose. Your gifts are some of the first things that come under attack by the world. In an effort to make the world more "uniform", we have slowly begun to eradicate uniqueness. Children have to be taught at an early age that their gifts don't make them weird, but that they in fact make them special. A failure to learn this about their gifts, will delay the process of sharpening them and sometimes stop the cultivation process altogether.

I heard an incredible story told by Sir Ken Robinson about Gillian Lynne. Mrs. Lynne is a british ballerina, dancer, actor, theatre director, and choreographer noted for her popular theatre choreography associated with the musical *Cats* and the current longest running show in Broadway history, *The Phantom of The Opera.* Apparently as a child, Gillian was very fidgety and often disruptive in class. If she would have been a child today, she would likely have been diagnosed as having ADHD (attention deficit hyperactivity disorder) and put on some sort of medication. In the 1930s, however, there was no such condition (It was first called hyperkinetic impulse disorder; the American Psychiatric Association (APA) formally recognized ADHD as a mental disorder in the late 1960s). Instead, the teacher recommended that her mother take her to see a therapist in order to get her to calm down.

During a meeting with the therapist, as Gillian sat on her hands fidgeting in her seat and being unresponsive to the questions, the therapist asked her mother to step outside with him so that he could speak with her in private. As they left the room, the therapist switched on the radio. Gillian's mother and the therapist watched from outside of the room, as Gillian began to get out her seat and dance as if her life depended on it. The therapist looked at Gillian's mother and said "Ms., there is nothing wrong with your daughter. She's a dancer. I suggest you enroll her in some dance classes."

Gillian would later say that the music made her come alive. She was placed in a dance class with children just like her; children who needed to move in order to think. She wasn't a "special needs child" or an "at risk youth". She was extremely gifted! She just needed to understand how she was created and the way her particular human machine was wired. She just needed to be allowed to be herself.

Because one young girl's gift was allowed the opportunity to breathe and then be properly cultivated, we have some of the most phenomenal dance choreography that the world has ever seen. That spark could have easily been put out if she had continued to be told that she was strange or if what burned inside of her and yearned to get out had never been allowed to.

We need each other. We all serve a purpose that lends itself to the enrichment of human life. We depend on this diversity of talent and God-given gifts in order to survive. I challenge you to look around you right now and imagine what life would be like if the things you use everyday were never created. What if those people had neglected their gifts and weren't able to create the things that we often take for granted? Now imagine how much greater the world would be if ALL of us embraced our gifts and talents and did our part to enrich human life; not just enrich it with inventions and technology, but with love, compassion, and generosity.

One of my favorite phrases is "No man is an island". We are all connected and intertwined and we depend on one another. Where one person is weak, the other is strong. Where one is impoverished, the other flourishes. Individually gifted for the collective good of the whole.

*Evening Meditation #4*

*Writers write, speakers speak, builders build, actors act, etc. Whatever your chosen pursuit, you must give yourself over to that with intention everyday. Talent is God-given but skill is honed every single day by diligent effort.*

*Repeat Aloud:*

*"I will do what I love and I love what I do. I do this because it is who I am. The world is better because I walk confidently in the direction of my God-given pursuit. My gift has finally been unwrapped and I will let it breathe"*

## 5

## *A Life Without Limits*

*"Look at all the possibilities rushing by you. The skies change, the clouds move. Look at all the possibilities rushing by you"*

*- Outputmessage on Quantum Love*

One day an old farmer came across a baby eagle that had fallen out of its nest. He couldn't bring himself to just leave the eagle there, so he picked it up and took it back to his farm. The only thing he knew to do was to place the eagle in the chicken coop with the chickens. After a while, as the eagle began to grow, it became too large for the coop; so the farmer called a friend of his to see if maybe he could take the eagle off of his hands. His friend was a wildlife enthusiast and the farmer was sure that he would be able to find the eagle a home.

The farmer's friend came over to the farm the next day. Before they went to the back of the house to see the bird, the farmer told his friend, "Before we go back here I need you to understand one thing. The eagle has been in the coop with the chickens for so long that it thinks it's a chicken.". "What do you mean?", asked the farmer's friend? "Well", the farmer said, "It clucks like the rest of the chickens, it eats the chicken feed, and it won't fly". "Impossible", said the friend.

As they approached the coop, the farmer's friend was shocked by what he saw. The old farmer was right. This huge bird was acting exactly like a chicken! It was clucking, eating the chicken feed, and its wings were tucked into its sides in a refusal to spread. The friend thought to himself, "I'm gonna change this. I mean, this just isn't right; king of the birds acting like a chicken?!" So the friend took the bird up on the roof of the chicken coop. He said to the eagle, "You are an eagle! You have been magnificently and wonderfully made. You were not created to live in a coop and eat chicken feed. You were made to fly! Now fly to your destiny!" He threw the eagle off of the roof of the coop. Both he and the farmer watched as the eagle simply fell back down to the ground and began walking around once again, clucking like a chicken. "I told you", said the farmer. "It thinks it's a chicken". "I'm not giving up on it that easy", said the friend.

So he picked the eagle up and put it in his truck. He drove down the road and found a tree. He climbed the tree with the bird in his hand. When he reached one of the low hanging branches, he perched the eagle on the branch and said "You are an eagle! You have been magnificently and wonderfully made. You were not created to live in a coupe and eat chicken feed. You were made to fly! Now fly to your destiny!" He pushed the eagle off of the branch. This time, the eagle fluttered its wings gently but quickly tucked them back into its side as it approached the ground.

Frustrated, but undaunted, the friend picked the eagle up and got back in his truck. He looked at the eagle and said, "Today you will become an eagle or you will die trying". He drove to a nearby cliff. He walked to the edge of the cliff, his own heart pounding as he felt the panic in the bird. He looked at the eagle and said, "You are an eagle! You have been magnificently and wonderfully made. You were not created to live in a coupe and eat chicken feed. You were made to fly! Now fly to your destiny!" With a deep breath and a heavy heave, he launched the eagle off of the cliff. He watched as the eagle did nothing but struggle to adjust itself in the air. His heart began to sink as he thought about what he had done. He was only trying to help the eagle find its identity but he has killed it in the process. He forced another look down at the eagle as it approached the sharp rocks below. Suddenly the eagle unfolded its wings from its side and struggled to spread them. A gust of wind forced its way into the eagle's wings; then another gust, and another, and another. Finally the eagle flapped its wings. For the first time, it had felt its own power. At that moment it made a noise other than a cluck. It was the sound of an eagle. Without fear, the eagle flapped its wings and began to soar upward and outward towards the now setting sun. It had finally left the nest that it had fallen out of as a young bird and the coupe that it had grown up in. It was now on its way to explore the world. With all of its power now discovered and its purpose uncovered, it was ready to live the life that it was created to live.

A lot of us fell out of the nest as children or grew up in situations that turned us into chickens. The environment you grew up in has had an incredible hand in shaping who you have become. One thing's for sure, you don't have to be a prisoner to your environment. You have the ability to transform it. The only way to fulfill your purpose is to become aware of possibility. You have to begin the process of stepping outside of your comfort zone. Start by listening to that small, yet persistent voice on the inside of you that implores you to reach new heights, to be better, and to excel beyond your circumstance. That voice is important because it moves you to action. Once you realize that you belong in the sky, the ground will feel too puny and simple to stay there.

Your potential is locked away on the inside of you, but what you might not understand is that the key to that potential is located inside of you as well. The ability to be great and to begin the process of fulfilling your purpose is within you. You hold the key to unlocking your potential. You simply need to search yourself.

There is a popular true story about an American columnist and retired neurosurgeon. He is credited with being the first surgeon to successfully separate conjoined twins joined at the head. His biography was made increasingly popular by a movie that debuted in 2009 called *Gifted Hands*. He grew up in the inner-city of Detroit, Michigan in an impoverished neighborhood. His mother had very few resources and no real formal education. She, however, saw potential in her son and instilled in him the idea that anything is possible. In one story, he recalls dreaming of a career in medicine. His family was on medical assistance so they would have to wait long hours just to see one of the interns on duty. While waiting in the hospital, he would soak in his surroundings. He would listen to the doctors and nurses moving around, going about their duties, and would imagine that it was his name being called on the PA system.

The young boy was able to see beyond his current circumstances and view his potential. Rather than waiting on someone to pull him out of his situation, he pushed himself out of it. His ability to tap into his potential allowed him to meet squarely with his life's purpose by becoming the Director of Pediatric Neurosurgery at Johns Hopkins Hospital at age 33, and become famous for his ground-breaking work separating conjoined twins.

There are no such things as limitations. There are only perceived limitations; and as it relates to you and your life, the only perception that matters is yours. Your mind will fence you in if you allow it to. You have to climb higher so you can see over and beyond the trees. Persistent effort will result in you seeing, not what your life currently is, but what your life can ultimately become. Persistent effort means, not sitting back and waiting on your purpose to find you, but stretching your arms wide and running as fast as you can across the chasm of time to meet it where it is. Once you meet it, throw your arms around it and never let it go. It will take you on the ride that you have always waited for and success and greatness will be your co-pilots.

## *Morning Meditation #5*

*Destiny is ready for you, are you ready for it? You are bigger than your circumstance. For so long you have allowed your situation to diminish your power. It is time to take control of your life.*

### *Repeat Aloud*

*"Today I will do the thing that I am most afraid of. I will believe in myself even if no one else does. I will not continue to diminish my power by being afraid to make choices. It is my life and my choice and I will choose to live it on purpose."*

### *There Will Be Forks*

Life is a series of choices. God has given you all of the tools that you need to live a life of purpose. He's given you the ability to manifest things and bring them under your control. He's also given you a lifeline to connect to Him through prayer and meditation. It is up to you to decide whether or not to utilize these tools.

When I was a kid I was drawn to a popular series of children's books called *Choose Your Own Adventure*, made popular by Edward Packard in the 1980s. In these books, the reader had the ability to choose their own destiny. For example, readers would be trapped in the occasional time loop, forced to flip back and forth between two pages, until they achieved their desired outcome. Depending on what choice they made at the end of the chapter, there would be instructions as to what page they were to go to next. There, they would discover the outcome of their decision. Sometimes it ended in death or some major setback. Other times, it ended in glory; but ultimately, the choice was the reader's.

I never really knew why I was so drawn to these books, but our school librarian, Mrs. Pressler, always made sure to let me know when there was one in that I hadn't checked out yet. Now, as an adult, I see the eerie similarity between those books and the journey of humanity in this life. It is the relationship between our choices and our destiny that make life what it is. Actually living life and not just existing is what God wants for us. He has given us the power of choice and allowed us to become fully engaged, active participants in our humanity.

The power of choice becomes very clear during tough times. Funny things begin to happen when you are in bad situations. You begin to search for every opportunity to shift blame. I learned this firsthand when I was in the midst of a difficult moment in my life. I was alone in a cold, dark apartment with no heat, no bed, no car, no money and I was angry. My emotions shifted from feelings of hopelessness to feelings of self-pity. I felt so sorry for myself. I thought, "What a terrible situation I am in"; "Where are the people who have professed to be my friends?"; "Where is this God that I have pledged my life to?"

When you are wallowing around in self-pity, it starts at the ankles and works its way up to the knees. At first, you are just wading in it. Then, before you know it, you are up to your neck in it and you can't breathe. It stifles your growth and you feel as if the only recourse you have is to lash out. "If I could just find someone to blame it will make me feel better", is what I said to myself in the silence of my room; "If I could just find a concrete reason for why I'm in this situation, then I will feel better." The problem with blame is that it has to have a face, and the only one that I had to give it looked back at me in the mirror everyday. If I blamed that man in the mirror, I still had to live with him; I had to exist in his presence. I had to share in his guilt as I pointed my finger at him. I had to feel the pain of blame that would be placed on his shoulders. All of this was true, but I had no choice. He was the only one who could make me better. He was the only one who could pull me up out of the muck and the mire that was my current status in life. He knew me more intimately than anyone else and ultimately, he was the primary reason for my problems.

Our EGO manipulates us into believing that people, things, worldly injustice, social prejudices, stereotypes, and other external forces are the primary source of our pain. It tricks us into fighting a fight that we cannot win. It takes away our power; because one thing we can't do, is control other people. Our power lies in our ability to be masterful in the operation of our own unique human being. Obstacles will appear from external places but the amount of subsequent pain and heartache that they cause is a direct reflection of the state of our internal self. Choice is a powerful word but an even more powerful action.

Life is a series of forks in the road. Certain decisions will lead you closer to your ultimate purpose and some will lead you away from it, but it is your decision which way you will go. Here is the good news, you have "Spiritual GPS". You just have to turn it on and trust it. Breathe in deeply and feel the presence of God swell up in your lungs. Open your eyes wide and allow the sun to shine into them. Place your hand on your chest and feel the rhythm of your heartbeat. You will find God in these moments and He will instill a sense of purpose and direction inside of you but He will not force you to choose righteously. He will not force you to do what your spirit tells you. He will not force you to be moral in your judgements; that decision is yours and yours alone.

## Evening Meditation #5

*You are not the artist, you are the canvas. This is a very important concept to understand. You are a reflection of God's plan. What would happen if, instead of forcing your agenda for today, you took some time to sit and receive instruction from God for what He would have you do. Sit silently until an action settles into your spirit. If you spend the time and God doesn't plant a seed of action in your heart for today, give yourself permission to go on with your day as planned. This exercise shows God where your priorities reside and it will open up a whole new world of possibilities. You will truly begin a "spirit-led" journey.*

*6*

## *Communicating With God - It's Not a Monologue*

*"The single biggest problem in communication is the illusion that it has taken place."*

*- George Bernard Shaw*

The essence of what this book is, lies in the essential understanding that each human is a spiritual incarnate. There is a piece of God in each one of us. We were created in His image with His essence. Because of this, our communication with God should be non-stop. If God lives on the inside of all of us, there should be no time when we do not feel his presence. It is like having your own personal control tower. The source who guides you through life and lands you safely on your purpose path, is available to you 24/7. He doesn't take the night off and He doesn't take sick days.

My favorite times as a kid were during the holidays. For my family, it didn't matter what Holiday it was, the focus was always on the meal that was going to be prepared. It was our tradition that the oldest member of the family would be the one to bless the food. This was usually either my Grandmother or my Great Aunt; neither of which were short-winded when it came to prayer. It was one of my favorite parts of the whole dinner, not because I was so excited to give thanks for the food, but because it was hilarious to me to watch the looks on my family member's faces as they waited impatiently for these "old ladies" to finish praying so that they could dig into the food. I always knew that I could count on my youngest aunt to be the first to give a disgruntled look. She was usually the one who had done the majority of the organizing and running around during the day, trying to make sure that dinner went off without a hitch. At this point, she was starving. Next, was my brother and my younger cousin; but the looks on their faces were similar to mine. They had one eye closed and the other open looking around to see who they could laugh at.

Finally, after what seemed like half an hour of prayer, we were ready to eat. This went on the majority of my childhood at every Holiday dinner. We rarely complained out of respect for the matriarchs of the family but truth be told, we really didn't get it. That's how it was though. We talked to God either when we were thankful for something that He had given us or when we needed something from Him. That's the way I thought it should be. I was taught that you shouldn't just talk to God when you want something; that thankfulness should be the main reason you pray. Although this was more than most of us were taught as children, it was still only a small part of what it means to communicate with God.

I would see my mom praying all of the time when I was young. When I was between 6 and 7 years old, it seemed as though she prayed non-stop. I didn't realize at that point what she was praying for but I would find out later that it was because she was asking God to give her the means by which to build a house.

Now first, I want you to understand that my mother's income was extremely low. I remember when I was working at my paid internship following undergraduate school, I found one of my mother's old pay stubs in some of her things. She made less than half (in two weeks) of what I was currently making weekly on my internship.

One day when I was playing in the living room, I had overheard her speaking to one of her friends about the house. She had asked my mom why she wouldn't simply try to borrow the money from such and such lender or take on another job. I remember my mom saying, "God hasn't told me to do that yet." What did she mean? Did she honestly think God was going to yell down from heaven and tell her what to do? What she meant was that God was going to move on the inside of her and show her what she should do. She was waiting on God to speak to her spirit.

I never asked her how she received confirmation from God because to me it didn't matter. All that mattered in our family at that time was that this single mother, who was raising two boys and living on a very low income, was now overseeing the construction of a new house being built from the ground up.

She had spoken to God many times and she understood this one thing very well, prayer is a dialogue. You speak to God and you wait on Him to speak back. It's strange to me that we would give the courtesy of proper rebuttal to a stranger before we would give it to God.

You have to learn to be patiently urgent in your communication with God. The answer may not come when or how you expect it but that does not mean that you cease communication. Sometimes our lives have impaired our ability to communicate and to receive responses. Often the line of communication has been temporarily severed or blocked by something that you have placed ahead of your relationship with God. When you are able to remove things from your life that are taking up your time and bogging down your communication, you will begin to be able to have a deeper relationship with the source of all life.

The concept of "fasting" does not only apply to food. It is a sacrifice; it's giving up something in your life that is taking up room. It means to make room in your life so that God can pour into you the information that you desire. Its a measure of faith that shows consistent confidence in God's love for you.

## Morning Meditation #6

*Often times we talk too much and aren't efficient in our communication, either with the people in our lives or with God. Say what absolutely NEEDS to be said and face what NEEDS to be faced. Next, be patiently urgent and committed to receiving a response. Expect as much from God as He expects from you. Verbalize to God what it is that you thank him for and what you might need of Him. Tell Him how you want Him to work in your life and then give Him the courtesy and the opportunity to respond. This morning's meditation is for you to design. Have a conversation with God.*

## *A Perspective Shift*

I mentioned earlier that I didn't fully understand why we prayed so long before dinner when I was a child. The reason I didn't understand it was because, up to that point, I had never in my life missed a meal. That would all change drastically later in my life. I would eventually be made aware of what it was like to really struggle financially and emotionally. That struggle caused a rather significant "shift" in my perspective with regards to my communication with God.

I was out to lunch with a friend of mine last summer. She is a Christian, so when the food came I figured that she would have no problem with giving thanks to God for it. I have gained a pretty big affinity for praying, so I usually volunteer myself to do the honors when I'm out eating with someone. Not to mention, I was born and raised in the south so I was taught that it was a "gentlemanly" thing to do. This time, however, I decided to ask her if she wanted to give thanks for the food. She said, "Sure!". As we bowed our heads to pray this is what I heard, "God is great, God is good, let us thank Him for our food. By His grace we must be fed, give us Lord our daily bread. Amen". Now first, let me just say that there is no "right" or "wrong" way to pray. As a matter of fact, this in essence, is a great prayer. My question had more to do with how it was delivered. I simply asked, "What did you just say to God?" "What do you mean?", she said. "I mean, why did you say that to Him?" It was a serious question that I wanted to know the answer to. She said, "I always say that. What do you say to Him?" "It's always different", I said. "It's much like when you and I talk; we rarely talk about the same thing. I guess it just depends on what's currently going on in my life". "I never really thought about", she replied. "I guess it is just something I have been saying for so long that it has become a habit. Thanks for bringing it to my attention."

A couple of things happened in this situation. First, I was able to hear and listen to the voice inside of me that said "ask her if she wants to pray". Second, I was able to feel comfortable enough with her to open it up for discussion. With those two simple things, I was able to brighten her awareness and illuminate her mind to a whole new possibility when it came to communicating with God.

Now before I come off "holier than thou", I need you to understand that what took place came out of my own inability to properly communicate with God. Several years back, I found myself in a situation that I never thought in a million years I would be in. I was homeless and penniless. There is nothing more humbling than the feeling of spending the last dime to your name; to hand someone a crinkled up dollar bill for a package of trail mix and not knowing where your next meal after that was going to come from. Then, to not just have to do that once, but to do it countless times over the next days, weeks, months, and years.

It was following the first of these situations that I truly knew what it meant to be thankful for my food. When money, food, and shelter show up out of nowhere it can humble you in ways very few other things can. I knew that it was God looking out for me and doing His part to ensure my survival. When you continue to make every mistake in the world and repeatedly shoot yourself in the foot by making bad decisions, ignoring God's direction, allowing your EGO to lead and you are still able to sit down and receive some nourishment; that's when you will truly understand what it's like to be thankful. The experience of being homeless, without food, and without money has given me a true sense of gratitude for the things that I have.

I never said I was an easy learner. It took some rather traumatic experiences to finally shift my awareness, whereas it was a simple conversation with my friend, sharing my experiences, that elevated her level of awareness. She received insight from me because she allowed herself to be open to it. She understood that I was expressing myself from a place of love and not condemnation.

Its funny how things change. Now I am the one who is charged with going to God on behalf of the family at dinner time and now I am the long-winded one. Everytime I pray over my food, whether alone or with a group of people, I can see my grandmother standing over my shoulder with a huge smile on her face.

## Evening Meditation #6

*Albert Einstein subtly suggests that we should live our lives as though everything is a miracle. I suggest that you take heed to that advice. When you wake up you should say to yourself, "wow, what a miracle?" Then go about your day with a "miracle mindset". Believe that everything that happens, everyone that you encounter is a miracle. See the miraculousness in life and within the world around you. Learn to appreciate the small things. Talk to God about the small things as if He is your friend because, in actuality, He is the best friend that you will ever have.*

*Repeat Aloud:*

*"Today I am appreciative for everything that is in my life. I will talk to God because He is my friend. I will tell Him how awesome His creations are and I recognize myself as a part of the greatness that is life."*

## 7

## *Light Up The World*

*"You are the light of the world. A city set on a hill cannot be hidden. Nor do people light a lamp and put it under a basket, but on a stand, and it gives light to all in the house. In the same way, let your light shine before others, so that they may see your good works and give glory to your Father who is in heaven.*

*Matthew 5:14-16 ESV*

Awareness is perhaps the most important component of spirituality. It is this awareness of yourself as a spiritual being that science calls "The Hard Problem". Science cannot explain an "in body experience" or "The Voltron Epiphany" as I have termed it in previous chapters. It is only through this awareness of self that we can truly connect to God and only through our connection to God will we truly be able to impact the world.

I want you to sit still for a moment, close your eyes, and just notice yourself. Be still and focus on yourself. Try to block out everything that's going on around you and just be in the essence of who you are. Notice your breath and the rhythm of your heartbeat. Don't ask any questions, just commit to being an observer. Do you feel it? Can you see it? Can you hear it? That's YOU watching you. This phenomenon is what we have come to know as consciousness. Science cannot explain it and often times just dismisses it all together. The "Hard Problem" is the inner movie that is constantly playing in our minds. It is a movie and you are at the heart of it; having a constant voice-over narrative. That separation from your body when you become the "Watcher" is a phenomenon that modern science has yet to fully explain. This is because it's not scientific; it is spiritual. Science is objective and is like oil to water in its relationship to consciousness because consciousness is very much (up to this point) subjective. Consciousness is as fundamental to human existence as space, time, and mass; however, it is perhaps the most mysterious phenomenon in the universe.

The beginning of consciousness is awareness. It begins with a brief glimpse into self. After a while, you will be able to go deeper into this level of awareness and you will begin to see yourself for the beautiful creation that you really are. You will be able to catch a glimpse of God as you gain a deeper awareness of yourself. This is where communication with God can truly begin to take place at a greater and much deeper level. As you start to see yourself as magnificent and when you begin to discover that place where you can truly connect to God, you will no longer be able to be confined by the parameters of your city, your state, your circumstances, or even your mind.

The ability to transcend this physical space is not unique to sages and yogis. It is made available to all of us. You have to begin with noticing yourself. Be the watcher and observer of self first and then you will be able to expand your awareness of the world and have a deeper sense of your relationship to it.

Most of us go through life with a contracted awareness at best. The most accurate description I've heard of a contracted awareness came from Dr. Deepak Chopra. Dr.

Chopra stated that, "Having a contracted awareness is like walking through a dark room with a candle". You can only see what is directly in front of you--the things that are only a few inches away. The darkness causes you to bump into things over and over and sometimes even hurt yourself in the process. You view the entire room as a maze filled with obstacles. This affects your attitude, it affects your choices, and ultimately impacts the way you view your relationship to the room and other people and things in it. Having a contracted awareness makes it increasingly difficult to recognize the good in people. It becomes difficult to find the usefulness in relationships, in space, in time, and in the very air you breathe. You become self-consumed and all of your energy is constricted. You bruise easily when your awareness is in a state of contraction. What then begins to happen is that you place a barrier around yourself to protect you from the objects in the room or even worse, you stop going into the room altogether. You stop living life because you are afraid of the things that you cannot see.

Now lets move to the experience of having an expanded awareness. I define an expanded awareness as having *some* knowledge of your spiritual self. By the end of this book, you should have moved, at least, to a level of expanded awareness. Having an expanded awareness is like replacing the candle with a flashlight. Now, you are able to get a better view of the room. You can now see the intended use of the items that you had previously perceived as obstacles. You notice the chair that you bumped into. You can see that it has been made for sitting in and to give you rest; whereas before you could only see it as something that caused you pain. It was because you were unable to see it for what it was that your attitude towards it was jaded. The effect of an expanded awareness has a profound impact on your attitude, your choices, and the way you view yourself in relation to the room and the objects in it.

Finally, let's move into an even deeper level of awareness. This is what most spiritual teachers call pure consciousness. It is the complete understanding of your spirit as it relates to your body and mind. It is like being in a glass room where light shines in from all directions. You see nothing as an obstacle but only as possibility. It allows you to operate in a space where you label nothing as a problem, but only notice the solutions. Life is about your perception of what is happening. Be positive and expect things to be great. You will find that good things come not to those who wait, but to those who expect them.

We often stifle our own ability to succeed by believing that bad things are products of inevitability. Challenge yourself today to be aware of the potential good in every person, situation, and circumstance. There is always the potential for good. A dark room is only dark because there is an absence of light. Be the light that those situations need. It is far better to light a candle than to scream at the darkness.

*"An optimist may see a light where there is none, but why must the pessimist always run to blow it out?"*

*- Rene' Descartes*

The secret to *The Secret* is that as you expect these great things to happen in your life, the actions required to make them happen begin to take physical shape. It is impossible to have pure, positive thoughts, and have them act out in evil, negative behavior. When you change your thoughts, you change your actions. We've already discussed how the body is servant to the mind, even if sometimes an unwilling servant. If you focus your energy on positive thoughts and affirmations, your physical actions will begin to fall in line.

*"For I know the plans I have for you, says the Lord. They are plans for good and not for evil, to give you a future and to give you hope"*

*- Jeremiah 29:11*

## Morning Meditation #7

*Be present and keyed in on the experience of your life, not the accomplishment of it. Enjoy those moments that are wrapped up in each and everyday. This is when you will begin to be able to move into a place of deeper meaning and gratitude. Sometimes there are moments you miss that are fleeting and are gone with the wind before you know it. Catch these moments and hold on tight. Only let go of the moment when you've given all that you have to give to it and gotten all that you can out of it. Be in the experience of yourself. Self-awareness is where the "magic" happens.*

*Repeat Aloud:*

*"I am myself today. I see myself for who I am. I am grateful for this moment, for this breath, for this heartbeat. It is in my smallness that I am able to find my bigness and it's in my bigness that I am able to find my smallness. This is a moment that matters. I will cherish it and I will cherish myself as God cherishes me"*

### *Transcendence*

To begin to move into a place of pure consciousness you should first begin to evoke feelings of gratitude. This means focusing on the things that you already have. Gratitude moves your EGO out of the way. How can you not feel gratified if what you are noticing is your breath, your heartbeat, your life? You are alive. You exist. There should be very few things that get you more excited than just knowing that you are alive.

You can choose the information that you seek out, depending upon your state of awareness. It is your choice whether to focus on things that make you feel gratitude or whether you focus on things that cause you to feel pain. Your attitudes are like good soldiers marching to the beat of your spiritual awareness. They will go in the direction in which you tell them to.

If we committed ourselves to personal transformation and a deeper level of self awareness, the world would be completely changed. Every major religion, before it was made into a "Dogma" (a set of rules laid down by authority figures to be incontrovertibly true), has at its core, a figure who has reached a level of pure consciousness. These teachers had a transcendent experience of some sort. Swiss psychiatrist and psychotherapist Carl Jung, believed these experiences to be journeys of transformation which he called "Individuation". He believed this to be at the heart, or as he described it, the "Mystic Heart" of all religions. It is the journey to meet yourself and at the same time meet the Divine.

If I had one wish in life, it would be to sit in on a conversation between Jesus and Buddha. I wonder what they would think about religion today? Would Buddha be able to recognize the God in Jesus and would Jesus be able to see the incredible ability of Buddha to tap into his "God Consciousness"?

Before Jesus and Buddha were lights unto the world, they needed to become lights unto themselves. Jesus' development into the Christian Messiah took Him most of His young adult life. He had to first embrace who He truly was and what He was truly sent to do before He could begin His earthly ministry (Which we believe to have lasted roughly 3 years).

Before Buddha could become the enlightened being that we believe him to have been and before he ever reached a state of pure consciousness, he had to begin the process of self-awareness. It was this awareness of himself that enabled him to enlighten his followers and inspire generations of people after him to seek out that same level of awareness.

Depending on who you talk to, the differences between these two great teachers vary greatly. A lot of their fundamentals were the same however. At the root of what they both believed were these 4 basic ideas; *awareness, gratitude, love, and compassion*. These 4 ideas are not only inherently powerful in what they enable, but also in what they disable. They disable and disarm the weapons of spiritual destruction;

anger, guilt, shame, regret, jealousy, and self-doubt. Awareness breeds gratitude, gratitude enables you to see the love that God has for you. This allows you to transmit His love through yourself and pour it out onto the world in the form of compassion.

My hope is that one day, we will remove our focus from the differences among religions and focus on the common threads that bind them. The common, life changing elements of awareness, gratitude, love, and compassion are necessary tools for harmony and peace in this life.

*Evening Meditation #7*

*True learning comes from a focused introspection. To learn yourself and to get to know who you are is to become more familiar with the one who created you. How do you know what food to feed your pet? How do you know in what soil or during which season to plant a seed for the best crop? You have to observe and learn intimately. Inasmuch, how do you expect to know how to nourish yourself for proper growth if you don't spend time gaining a deep self-awareness. Take time and explore your own spirit. Fill yourself up so much with God's love that it will spill out onto everyone around you.*

*Repeat Aloud:*
*"I am God's love manifested in human form. He fills me up and when I have had my fill, I will pour all of it out onto the world so that I might have room to receive more"*

## 8

## *Living to Die or Dying to Live? - How will you spend life?*

*"Dream as if you'll live forever. Live as if you'll die today."*

*-James Dean*

*"I went to the woods because I wished to live deliberately, to front only the essential facts of life, and see if I could not learn what it had to teach, and not, when I came to die, discover that I had not lived"*

*- Henry David Thoreau*

The essence of life is growth. Everything grows; from the flowers in the ground, to the fish in the sea, to the birds in the air. Everything has its existence rooted in growth. The question is, what will you have produced at the end of your growing? Life is a choice between a long baptism and a sprinkle every now and then. It is better to live a life of immersion than to live untouched. If there is any fear in your life, it should be the fear of not giving it your all. Your job is not to be perfect or to even strive for perfection. Perfection, in itself, is subjective. Your job is to be the most abundant and unapologetic form of YOU. It is to live in a space where none of your talent is wasted on trivial things. Your hope should be to wake up every morning knowing that you gave it your all yesterday and today will be no different.

This is the time of expansion. Identify your gifts and seek with all your might to expand them and stretch them as wide as you can possibly stretch them. Lend your gifts to tasks that make you nervous. Lend your gifts to situations that challenge you. Lend your gifts to things that you have never attempted in your life. Stretch, stretch, stretch your gifts until they become so strong that you will be unwilling and unable to pull them back. They will exist in a space more vast and wider than you would have ever imagined, and your effect on the world will be profound. This is the call on your life. To reach your own human potential. Shatter the ceiling and push to the sky. Your objective is not to become who the world thinks you should become. Your objective is only to become yourself. Completely and fully develop into YOU. Trust, love, and focus on that person. No gifts can be given by you if you don't cultivate yourself enough so that you might have the ability to give and to serve.

Your word is your wand. Speak ,then become. Use your words as if every word out of your mouth is creating your destiny because it truly is. Speak health and prosperity into your life and the lives of those around you.

There are several things you can begin to do to assure that you are living a life of growth. Find these 3 things in your life: a mentor, a peer group, and someone to mentor. These 3 elements are essential to your growth.

Let's talk first about your mentor. Growth often comes about by learning from someone else's experiences. It's also important that you allow yourself to be challenged. Place people in your life that challenge you to be better and who hold you accountable to meet the requirements and standards that you have set for yourself.

Your peer group is essential as well. These are often the people that you spend the majority of your time with. If you look at the lives of the people who are closest to you, you will be able to predict the trajectory of your life based on how their lives are going. My mother used to say it like this, "son, watch the company you keep because the company you keep will keep you". I'm not saying that you should only associate with people that think just like you and agree with everything you do, but you should have friends that have your best interest at heart and believe in your purpose. Your morals should line up with their morals. Life is a team sport. Even Jesus chose 12 other men to "do life with".

Last, but not least, is the person you mentor. It will give you so much pleasure to help someone along their way. It just does something for the spirit when you do good and become a positive impact on someone else's life. World renowned speaker Jim Rohn once said "If you share knowledge with 10 people, they each heard it once but you will have heard it 10 times". Working with a mentee is self-medication. We never stop learning and sometimes we need things reiterated. I believe that you will be shocked to find out how much it helps your growth when you invest in the life of someone else.

Another thing you can do in your attempt to grow your life, is purchase a piece of artwork. Buy something that represents what you want your life to look like. It can be an abstract idea. It doesn't matter what other people see when they look at the art. All that matters is what you see and feel when you look at it. We all have an idea of the person that we want to become and if you've gotten this far in the book, you have an understanding of what God wants you to become and that you were created with a dynamic purpose. Look at the artwork everyday and let it remind you of the potential you have locked away inside of you. Be reminded of this spirit of potential that desperately wants to get out. Begin to feel yourself slowly embrace and even embody that vision that you see reflected and manifested in that piece of art. Become the canvas and allow the art to be painted into your life.

Bloom where you're planted. Don't wait for everything to be "perfect" before you take action towards fulfilling your purpose. Things will never be perfect. The imperfection is what makes triumph so great. Often times it is the aspect of overcoming that gives us a glorious victory. Snatch victory from the jaws of defeat. Take positive action and do what you can, where you are, with what you have. By doing this, you can actually begin to transform circumstances so that they become more favorable for you. Life is so much about how you take it. The one thing you can control is your perception of what is happening. Be positive and expect things to be great.

## Morning Meditation #8

*Who do you want to become? What does that look like? Visualize where you see yourself going, doing, and being. Become that even before you "become that". Dress the part, walk the part, talk the part. Prepare for your destiny but be excellent in the place you are. Wherever you find yourself in your life or your career, go above and beyond what is required of you for those particular places and tasks in your life. Your performance and mind set should not match up with where you are but they should belong to the status of where you are going. Don't sit back and wait on destiny. Once you see it approaching just over the horizon, drop what you are doing and run as fast as you can to go meet it and greet it with open arms. It will be happy to see you because it has been waiting on you even longer than you have been waiting on it.*

*Repeat Aloud:*

*"I will not use my life as a teaching tool for how to become mediocre. I deserve everything that life has to give me and I deserve to be a part of the greater good that is God's plan. I will not spend my life conforming to the opinions of those that doubt me. I see myself through a heavenly lense and through that lense is a clear vision of the life that I am destined to live"*

## *Do Not Cease Exploration*

As a teenager, I sang in the choir at my church. I discovered early that singing probably wasn't the thing that God wanted me to do with my life but it was fun and I could at least hold onto a note for a few seconds. Around the holidays, we would go visit the nursing homes and sing Christmas carols to the people who would be spending the holidays there; often times without any visits from family members.

Going to the nursing home was always a difficult thing for me. I told myself that it was because of the smell and how it was always way too cold or too hot, never anywhere in between. Truth be told, the real reason I disliked nursing homes was that because I would get this rush of emotion that would overcome me when I saw old people who could no longer care for themselves. I would have trouble getting through the visit because I would have this huge knot in my throat and a sinking feeling in the pit of my stomach. These symptoms were a prelude to the tears that would well up in my eyes.

I thought it was just the fact that they were probably close to death and I felt sympathy for them. After talking to several people in these nursing homes and having several family members of my own placed in them, I understood that the emotion I felt came from a different place. The reason the nursing homes felt uncomfortable to me was that it was a place shrouded with regret. The air was thick with the lost hopes and dreams of people who had not met with their potential in life and had resigned themselves to the fact that they might never have the opportunity to walk down their paths of purpose.

If you were to ask someone who is nearing their life's end to ponder over it, way too many of them will tell you that their regret about life is having never truly lived it. They lived out of fear, doubt, guilt, or shame and once their lives stopped growing they had very little to show for it by way of spiritual gratification.

Had I known then what I know now, I would have been able to share with them that their life's purpose was not over. That they still had so much to give to the world. Their stories helped shape my life and I'm sure that many others who were able to visit with them and hear their stories feel the same way.

God's time is not our time. He never thinks of you as useless. He will squeeze every ounce of potential out of you even if you spend your life working against it. My suggestion is that you work with God throughout the course of your life instead of working against Him.

*"You can either be a host to God or a hostage to your EGO"*

*- Dr. Wayne Dyer*

God never consults your past to create your future. Don't be a prisoner to your past. You can break through into your future by forgiving yourself and filling yourself with the understanding that God forgives you too. Learn from the past mistakes of your life, for the only true failure lies in the lack of learning. Let the knowledge propel you so far forward in your life that you will not even be able to look back upon those mistakes. They will become like tiny specks in the distance. Those mountains will now seem to be molehills distorted by the dust of your footsteps as you run towards your purpose.

You must view your purpose as a door that is locked and double bolted. It can only be opened and shut by you. No one else has the key, you have it! Get rid of all of the other useless keys you have attached to life's key chain and focus on the one key that has the word "purpose" inscribed on it.

The thing about living a life of purpose is that in order to meet with it, you have to know what it is. In essence, your purpose calls to you. It is your guiding light. It will lead you to where it lives. Purpose is like that friend on the phone giving you directions to their house. You might not see it at the moment but the belief that it is where it says it is, allows you to trust in its direction and continue your journey towards meeting it.

## Evening Meditation #8

*See your purpose, believe that it exists, and follow the path that it has laid down before you. Understand that this life is only for a brief moment and that's alright, because this moment, no matter how long or how brief, will be a moment filled with joy, happiness, and well-being if you choose it to be so.*

*Repeat Aloud:*

*"For this time, while I am wrapped in this skin, I will be the very best of God."*

*"We shall not cease from exploration, and the end of all our exploring will be to arrive where we started and know that place for the first time"*

*- T.S. Eliot*

**The End/Beginning...**

## *Epilogue*

When God places something before you, you don't have to manipulate the circumstances. Your true power comes from your honesty and integrity. The things that God has planned for your life, you cannot even begin to comprehend. You just have to be true to Him, true to yourself, and let your spirit lead. God loves you from the inside out. You owe it to yourself, to love yourself that exact same way.

**The Wisdom Tree**

*A Few*

*Words To Live By*

*"The essence of life is growth"*

*"Observation brings confirmation"*

*"Worry is praying for what you don't want"*

*"A man with no discipline has no direction"*

*"There is a call on your life to expand your gifts"*

*"Never judge past decisions based upon present information"*

*"No past regrets, no future sorrows. There is only this moment. We must nurture this moment and not let it slip past without care. This moment is where our power lies"*

***The Author…in his own words***

"I was created to write in some capacity; to uplift and to elevate to a heightened state of awareness. Therefore, I will do this to the best of my ability as long as I am in this strange space called 'LIFE'. Abundance in life, in love, and in wellness to all of you; always."

~ Justin Jamar

Made in the USA
Columbia, SC
19 May 2021